BIOGRAPHIES

GRETA THUNBERG

by Jaclyn Jaycox

PEBBLE
a capstone imprint

Published by Pebble, an imprint of Capstone
1710 Roe Crest Drive, North Mankato, Minnesota 56003
capstonepub.com

Library of Congress Cataloging-in-Publication Data is available on the
Library of Congress website
ISBN: 9781666350531 (hardcover)
ISBN: 9781666350746 (paperback)
ISBN: 9781666350708 (ebook PDF)

Summary: Discover the details you want to know about inspiring young
activist Greta Thunberg. You'll learn about the childhood, challenges, and
accomplishments of this young leader in the fight against climate change.

Editorial Credits
Editor: Mandy Robbins; Designer: Hilary Wacholz; Media Researchers:
Jo Miller and Pam Mitsakos; Production Specialist: Tori Abraham

Image Credits
Newscom: ZUMA Press/Claudio Bresciani / Tt, Cover, 1; Shutterstock: aapsky,
15, Alexandros Michailidis, 19, Dani Ber, 13, Daniele COSSU, 10, Drop of
Light, 18, Ink Drop, 25, lev radin, 5, 21, Liv Oeian, 14, 29, Marco Ciccolella, 27,
Noah Labinaz, 22, Oleksiy Mark, 7, Per Grunditz, 17, Rich Carey, 9, Roland
Marconi, 23, Thomas Barrat, 12

All internet sites appearing in back matter were available and accurate when
this book was sent to press.

Table of Contents

Words in **bold** are in the glossary.

Who Is Greta Thunberg?

Greta Thunberg is an **activist**.
At just 15 years old, she began to
fight **climate change**. The world is
heating up. Snow and ice are melting.
Oceans are rising. Weather is getting
more extreme. Greta didn't wait for
change. She took action.

Greta began to **protest** alone.
What happened next surprised her.
She started a worldwide movement.
Now she travels around the world.
She speaks to leaders. She demands
change.

Greta holding her protest poster

Growing Up Greta

Greta was born January 3, 2003, in Stockholm, Sweden. She lived with her mother, father, and younger sister, Beata.

Kids bullied Greta at school. It was hard for Greta. She hid during recess. She came home crying every day. Greta's family was worried. They hoped school would get better for her. But it got worse.

Stockholm, Sweden

In fifth grade, Greta's teacher showed the class a movie. It was about climate change. It showed the effects it has on Earth. Greta saw **polluted** oceans. She saw extreme weather events. She saw starving animals. This film changed Greta forever.

Greta's classmates went on as usual. But Greta couldn't. Her sadness grew. She stopped talking. She hardly ate. Greta lost a lot of weight. She almost ended up in the hospital.

Polluted ocean water and a sea turtle

Greta's parents took her to many doctors. In 2015, they found out she has Asperger's syndrome. Greta thinks differently than most people. She is very smart. But it's not easy for her to talk to people. It's hard for her to make friends. She often focuses on just one thing. Greta's focus is on fighting climate change.

Greta says having Asperger's isn't a bad thing. She's called it a superpower. It drove her to fight for change.

Family Life

Greta's family has always supported her. They helped bring her out of her sadness. Her father learned about climate change. The family made changes to help the **environment**. They stopped eating meat. They started growing their own vegetables. They put **solar panels** on their home.

A vegetable garden

solar panels

Solar panels use energy from the sun.
They create electricity. Power plants
pollute the air. Solar panels don't.

Greta's mother is a singer. She performed around the world. In 2016, Greta's mother decided to stop flying for her work. Airplanes release gases into the air. These gases can add to climate change. It upset Greta when her mother traveled by airplane.

Greta's mother, Malena Ernman

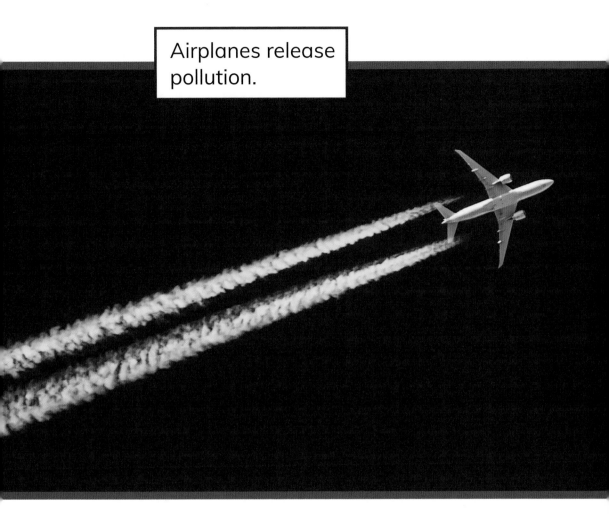

Airplanes release pollution.

These changes made Greta feel better. But hers was just one family. More needed to be done. She decided to get the attention of her government.

Fighting for Change

In 2018, Greta began to protest. She planned a strike over summer break. Her dad helped her make a sign. It read, "School Strike for Climate." On August 20, Greta skipped school. She stood alone outside a government building all day. She continued to do this every Friday.

After a few weeks, people joined her. Word quickly spread about this young activist. The movement became known as Fridays for Future. By December, students around the world were protesting too.

Greta during her "School Strike for Climate"

In December 2018, Greta spoke at the United Nations (UN) Climate Change Conference. She urged leaders to take climate change seriously. She continued speaking at as many gatherings as she could. She worked with scientists. They made sure her facts were correct.

The United Nations building in New York City

Greta speaks to adults at the UN Climate Change Conference.

Greta's speeches were powerful. She didn't hide how upset she was at world leaders. She told them adults should be taking care of the problem. But they weren't.

Greta received support from people everywhere. In March 2019, she was nominated for a Nobel Peace Prize. In the end, she didn't win. But she was the youngest person to ever be nominated.

In 2019, Greta did her schoolwork online. She wanted to focus more on her activism. In August 2019, she headed to New York City. She traveled by a solar-powered boat. The trip took two weeks.

Greta on the solar-powered boat

Greta spoke to world leaders again. On September 20, she went to the New York City Global Climate Strike. She led a march in the streets. But it wasn't just in New York. Millions of people marched in 185 countries. It was the largest climate protest in history.

New York City's Global Climate Strike

Greta speaks at the New York City Global Climate Strike.

In December 2019, Greta was recognized for her work. She was named *TIME* magazine's "Person of the Year." She is the youngest person to ever receive this honor.

The Greta Effect

Climate change is far from being solved. But because of Greta, it is being talked about much more. She has inspired people around the world. This has been called "The Greta Effect." Many people are making changes to help the planet.

In October 2020, *I Am Greta* was released. This movie shows Greta's daily life. It follows her on her journey to fight climate change.

Protestors in London march to end climate change.

Not everyone supports Greta. Some people disagree with her. They include world leaders. But she doesn't let anyone stop her.

Greta continued her work at home during the COVID-19 **pandemic**. She held online events. She met with leaders through video.

In September 2021, Greta got back out there. She led her first Fridays for Future protest in more than a year. She plans to continue this fight for as long as she lives.

Greta speaks at a Fridays for Future rally in northern Italy in 2021.

Important Dates

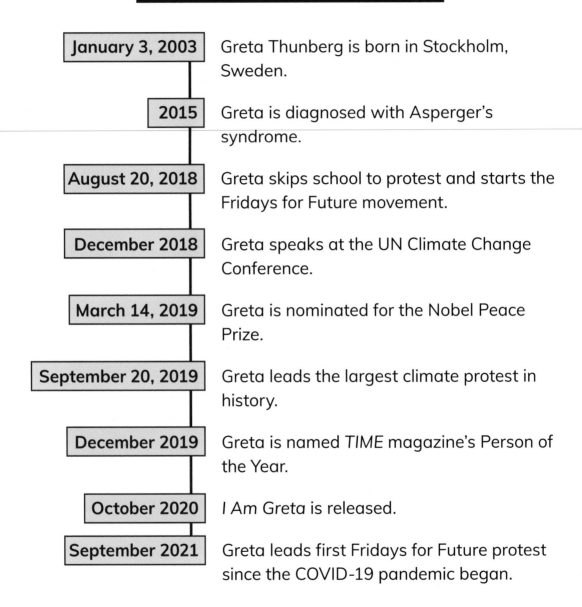

January 3, 2003	Greta Thunberg is born in Stockholm, Sweden.
2015	Greta is diagnosed with Asperger's syndrome.
August 20, 2018	Greta skips school to protest and starts the Fridays for Future movement.
December 2018	Greta speaks at the UN Climate Change Conference.
March 14, 2019	Greta is nominated for the Nobel Peace Prize.
September 20, 2019	Greta leads the largest climate protest in history.
December 2019	Greta is named *TIME* magazine's Person of the Year.
October 2020	*I Am Greta* is released.
September 2021	Greta leads first Fridays for Future protest since the COVID-19 pandemic began.

Fast Facts

Name:
Greta Thunberg

Role:
climate change activist

Life dates:
January 3, 2003, to present

Key accomplishments:
Greta Thunberg travels the world fighting climate change. She speaks to world leaders. She leads protests around the globe. She has inspired millions of people to do their part.

Glossary

activist (AK-tuh-vist)—a person who works for social or political change

climate change (KLY-muht CHAYNJ)—a significant change in Earth's usual weather over a period of time

environment (in-VY-ruhn-muhnt)—the natural world of the land, water, and air

pandemic (pan-DEM-ik)—a disease that spreads over a wide area and affects many people

pollute (puh-LOOT)—to make something dirty or unsafe

protest (PRO-test)—to speak out about something strongly and publicly

solar panel (SOH-lur PAN-uhl)—a flat surface that collects sunlight and turns it into power

Read More

Neuenfeldt, Elizabeth. *Greta Thunberg: Climate Activist*. Minneapolis: Bellwether Media, Inc., 2022.

Peterson, Megan Cooley. *Understanding Climate*. North Mankato, MN: Pebble, 2021.

Winter, Jeanette. *Our House Is on Fire: Greta Thunberg's Call to Save the Planet*. New York: Beach Lane Books, 2019.

Internet Sites

Greta Thunberg Facts!
natgeokids.com/uk/kids-club/cool-kids/general-kids-club/greta-thunberg-facts/

Speaking Up for Earth
timeforkids.com/g2/speaking-up-earth-2/

Greta Thunberg Facts for Kids
kids.kiddle.co/Greta_Thunberg

Index

About the Author

Jaclyn Jaycox is a children's book author and editor. When she's not writing, she loves reading and spending time with her family. She lives in southern Minnesota with her husband, two kids, and a spunky goldendoodle.